Mobil New Zealand Nature Series

NEW ZEALAND NATIVE TREES 2

Mobil New Zealand Nature Series

NEW ZEALAND NATIVE TREES 2

Nancy M. Adams

REED

Published by Reed Books, a division of Octopus Publishing Group (NZ) Ltd, 39 Rawene Road, Birkenhead, Auckland. Associated companies, branches and representatives throughout the world.

ISBN 0 7900 0246 9

First published 1983
Reprinted 1991

Printed in Singapore

Contents

Foreword

FEW PEOPLES have come to hold their native vegetation in such esteem as have New Zealanders; yet few peoples can have destroyed their native flora so vigorously and rapidly in converting what was once richly forested land to agricultural uses. Fortunately, even while this was happening to New Zealand, legislators had the good sense to reserve fairly large areas as national parks, scenic and other reserves, and state forests. Most of these parks, reserves, and forests serve the essential purpose of preventing erosion and helping to absorb some of the heavy rainfall of the mountain lands, so reducing the intensity of flooding.

Many New Zealanders enjoy recreation and sport in these places and take pride in knowing something of the plants that make up the natural vegetation. For such people, Nancy Adams provides here, with accuracy and artistry, the details of some of the commoner trees.

A. L. Poole
Former Director-General of Forests
New Zealand

Introduction

FEW PLACES IN NEW ZEALAND are far from "the bush". In most of these areas of native forest, some of which cover many hectares, the types of forest that once covered the country may still be seen in something like their primitive state.

In the simplest terms these forests are classified into "podocarp-mixed broadleaf", "kauri", or "beech" forests, the names indicating the types of trees that are either the most conspicuous or the most abundant in their composition.

Podocarp-mixed broadleaf forests are those in which there are numerous tall trees belonging to the family Podocarpaceae, i.e., rimu, kahikatea, matai, miro, silver pine and totara. They are all softwood timber trees, some with the alternative names of red, white, black and silver pine. Growing with them are many kinds of "broadleaf" hardwood trees such as kamahi, tawa, kohekohe, rata, and many others that form a leafy canopy above which stand the tops of the tall podocarps. Also included under this heading are: swamp forests with dense stands of kahikatea; forests of some dry areas where totara is the most abundant tree; high-altitude forest with kaikawaka (cedar); and coastal forest with many "broadleaf" species but few podocarps.

Apart from the magnificent trees in this type of forest there are many shrubs, tree-ferns, lianes and an abundance of small ferns, mosses and lichens. Few trees are without epiphytes, which are perching plants that use the host tree for a place to grow upon but not for nourishment, as do parasites such as mistletoe. The epiphytes are of many kinds, ranging from tree species — rata, puka and others that germinate in pockets of humus high in the branches of large trees — to shrubs, astelias, orchids and ferns. In forest where the rainfall is high the epiphytes may be so numerous as to make the identification of their host tree difficult. Mossy growths cover the trunks and paint-like lichens disguise the bark. When the trees grow too high for flowers and fruit to be gathered, an examination of fallen leaves, petals and fruits will give an indication of the trees in the vicinity.

Kauri forest of the north of the North Island is similar to the podocarp-mixed broadleaf forest, but with the kauri as a frequent tree. Broadleaf trees are abundant in such forests, together with other trees and shrubs that do not grow further south than the kauri.

The exterior view of kauri forest is characterised by the tall kauris that stand well above the surrounding trees. High in their branches are huge clumps of perching plants. Within the forest the undergrowth is dense with "cutty grass", scrambling kiekie, shrubs and ferns. Tall nikau palms and tree-ferns reach up to the forest canopy, and taraire, tawa, toatoa and towai are common trees. The enormous trunks of the kauri are covered with flaking bark that piles in mounds encircling the bases of the trunks. Flaking and peeling bark discourages the growth of epiphytes on the trunks of kauri and other trees such as miro, matai, rimu and totara.

Beech forests are those in which one or more species of southern beech grow in quantity. Except in mountain regions or in very dry beech forest, podocarps and broadleaf trees are found in amongst the beech, often in gullies and valleys.

Beech forest is very different in appearance from the other forests. The beech trees are usually of a fairly uniform height with a dense leaf canopy; a soft green light filters through their foliage to the mosses and ferns on the forest floor. Epiphytes and lianes are few, and the place of an understorey of trees is taken by beech saplings and a few species of small-leaved shrubs. Where beech grows on dry hillsides the forest floor may have only a covering of fallen leaves and patches of white or yellow-brown moss. Twiggy shrubs form a sparse undergrowth. In very wet regions beech trees are moss-clad and rise from a spongy carpet of moss and filmy ferns. Large clumps of mistletoe, either scarlet or yellow-flowered, are a feature of beech forest in summer.

To make a study of native trees does not mean an excursion to remote and untouched areas of forest. Throughout New Zealand there are many large and small patches and pockets of native vegetation where a number of different trees may be seen.

Native trees on farmland are often an indication of the forest that once covered the district. Such groves of trees are useful in providing shelter and shade for stock, at the same time giving a pleasant aspect to pasture land. In northern farmland puriri and taraire are handsome shade trees. Totara, kahikatea, beech, cabbage trees, manuka and kanuka are seen in many districts. Karaka, ngaio and pohutukawa flourish near the coast, while in inland places beech, ribbonwood and fuchsia are common.

Remnants of native bush are often found alongside rivers and streams, especially in steep-sided gorges. Kowhais and lacebarks are particularly beautiful along riverbanks and along the shores of lakes and inlets. In the north, pohutukawa is a tree of the shoreline, while in some southern areas rata is a coastal tree. Even on barren, windswept coasts, gullies running back from the shore may be a rewarding collecting ground for small trees.

Large areas of hill country and poor land are often covered with manuka scrub and the taller kanuka. In the shelter beneath manuka, seedlings of some forest trees flourish and soon appear above the manuka. In the north, kauri, tanekaha and rewarewa are conspicuous on manuka country where there once was forest. Other small, quick-growing trees that are early members of a "second growth" bush are mahoe, wineberry, rangiora, five-finger and karamu.

Because many of the best-known tall forest trees have been illustrated in *Native Trees I*, emphasis is given here to some of the smaller trees of more open country. In many places there are roads that ascend through the forest to the shrub and tussock at and above the bush-line. Some of the trees most likely to be found within reach of these roads have been chosen — hakeke, mountain toatoa, neinei, inaka, the mountain cabbage tree and ribbonwood.

A selection of coastal and forest trees from both northern and southern localities is included as well as examples from dry, open country such as matagouri and dwarf kowhai.

Notes on text and plates

THE TREES appear in the same order in which they may be found in standard, recent botanical reference books — a natural order of classification based upon their relationship to each other. Latin and plant family names as well as common names are given.

To use the Latin name is the only certain way of referring to any plant, as common names are often shared by several plants, sometimes quite dissimilar in character. Some plants have several common names which vary from district to district. The Latin names are international; any botanist would immediately recognise the plant described when he or she knows its Latin generic and specific names which together may be given to no other plant in the world.

N.M.A.

Mamuku

Sphaeropteris medullaris (Forst. f.) Bernh.
Family: Cyatheaceae

MAMUKU, the black tree fern, is probably the best known of the native tree ferns. It grows to a height of at least 15m, and in many places it soars above the surrounding trees to spread its huge umbrella of pale green fronds. In places where the forest has been cut over, mamuku is one of the first plants to regenerate on the more shaded slopes. In heavy bush it is confined to steep gullies, streamsides and the forest margins.

Mamuku is distinguished from the other tall tree ferns by its black trunk patterned with diamond-shaped scars that remain after the old fronds have dropped off.

Mamuku (previously placed in the genus *Cyathea*) grows in most parts of New Zealand, but is absent from colder, drier South Island localities.

Plate 1

cm

Nikau

Rhopalostylis sapida Wendl. & Drude
Family: Palmae (Arecaceae)

NIKAU is the only native member of the palm family. It is tall growing, up to 20m, with a slender trunk banded with the scars of fallen fronds. These dark green fronds each have a broad sheathing base fitting tightly around the growing point at the top of the trunk. The branched inflorescences emerge from between the leaf sheaths and bear many small pinkish-cream flowers that are followed by the bright scarlet fruits.

Nikau grows in the warmer parts of the country, particularly in coastal forests. In places where this forest has almost disappeared groves of tall nikau palms remain.

Ti – Cabbage Tree

Cordyline australis (Forst. f.) Endl.
Family: Agavaceae

CABBAGE TREES are one of the most distinctive features of the New Zealand landscape. They grow in all parts of the country extending from the coast to the foothills of the ranges. They are said to be an indication of fertile ground and particularly favour the alluvial soils of flood plains, swamps and lakesides. They are plants of open places where they may form large groves often of ancient many-headed trees surrounded by their progeny.

The large, much-branched flower heads appear in late spring, in some seasons on almost every leafy "cabbage". The small, creamy-white flowers have an especially beautiful scent in the warm air. They are followed by small, speckled, whitish berries that are widely spread by birds.

Cabbage trees may reach a height of about 20m, but as they grow older they increase in girth and the trunks become massive, buttressed and often hollow. These cavities may be the home of birds, bats and sometimes swarms of wild bees.

Plate 3

Toi-i – Mountain Cabbage Tree

Cordyline indivisa (Forst. f.) Steud.
Family: Agavaceae

TOI-I or mountain cabbage tree is one of the most handsome plants in the New Zealand flora. Individual plants may reach a height of 8m, but they are often much shorter and grow in dense clumps in mountainous country where there is a high rainfall. The leaves are wide, very glossy and dark green with a conspicuous mid-rib. The flowers are borne in a stout inflorescence that hangs down just below the crown of leaves. They are dull pink and followed by purplish-blue berry-like fruits.

Toi-i, a plant of damp mountain forest margins, may be seen where roads climb up to the bush line, particularly on Mount Egmont and Mount Ruapehu. It grows south of the Thames ranges and throughout the South Island, especially in Westland and Fiordland.

Plate 4

cm

Mountain Toatoa

Phyllocladus alpinus Hook. f.
Family: Podocarpaceae*

MOUNTAIN TOATOA or celery-leaved pine may reach a height of about 8m but is very often a dense, sometimes low-growing shrub especially at higher altitudes. It is a plant of open places on the mountains, but also occurs in subalpine forest and in some places on the West Coast and Southland is found at sea level.

In common with tanekaha and the lowland toatoa (see *Trees I*) mountain toatoa has no true leaves but has somewhat rhomboid, flattened, leaf-like branchlets (cladodes). The foliage is dull, bluish-green and very aromatic. The male flowers are in small terminal clusters and the female on the margins of the cladodes.

Mountain toatoa is more plentiful above 500m altitude in mountains south of the Coromandel Peninsula where the rainfall is plentiful, although it is absent from Mount Egmont and Stewart Island.

* A recent revision of the celery-leaved pines in Australasia and Malesia has resulted in their being placed in a special family, Phyllocladaceae. The New Zealand mountain toatoa is considered to be a variety of the Tasmanian *P. aspleniifolius* and is now *P. aspleniifolius* (Labill.) Hook. f. var. *alpinus* (Hook. f.) H. Keng.

Plate 5

cm

Horopito

Pseudowintera colorata (Raoul) Dandy
Family: Winteraceae

HOROPITO is a small, very colourful tree up to 10m high found in forests and scrub at higher altitudes. In areas where frosts are severe it assumes bright reddish-bronze foliage. Mountain horopito leaves are yellow-green blotched with red and purple, the under side of the leaf is pale with a pattern of tiny dots. The foliage is aromatic and very peppery to the taste. The flowers are small and borne in the axils of the leaves; they are followed by dark, blue-black berries.

Mountain horopito is found in the high country from the Mamakus to Stewart Island and is particularly noticeable on the western side of the Volcanic Plateau, on Banks Peninsula and on the Otago Peninsula.

Plate 6

Taraire

Beilschmiedia tarairi (A. Cunn.) Kirk
Family: Lauraceae

TARAIRE is a heavily foliaged tree reaching 20m that usually grows in groves unmixed with other kinds of trees. The large, rounded, very dark green leaves form a dense canopy that allows little light to penetrate to the forest floor, which is therefore rather bare and covered with a crisp carpet of dry, brown leaves. The flowers are insignificant, but the large purple berries are very handsome and readily seen.

Taraire is a tree of northern areas reaching its southern limit at East Cape. It is now rather local in occurrence as farms have encroached on the fertile lands it previously occupied and the kauri forests where it formed an understorey have largely vanished.

Plate 7

cm

Kotukutuku

Fuchsia excorticata (J.R. & G. Forst.) Linn. f.
Family: Onagraceae

KOTUKUTUKU or tree fuchsia is one of the few native trees that is almost completely deciduous, particularly in the South Island. When the fuchsia is bare in winter, the very distinctive pinkish tone of the trunks and branches and the peeling, papery bark is conspicuous. The native fuchsia may reach a height of 10-12m although on exposed hillsides it is much shorter. The leaves are very soft with pale undersides; the flowers, although inconspicuous, are quite brightly coloured especially when the anthers shed their extraordinary blue pollen. The fruits are large, succulent purple berries.

The tree fuchsia is found throughout New Zealand from sea level to the upper limit of the forest and is a plant of bush margins and streamsides. It is now one of the commonest trees forming a hedge where roads have been cut through bush areas.

Plate 8

cm
mm

Tutu

Coriaria arborea Lindsay
Family: Coriariaceae

TUTU is a common shrub or small tree reaching 5m in height with several rather soft stem-like trunks and angular branches bearing glossy, dark green leaves. The small flowers are produced on long, pendant inflorescences and are followed by small succulent purplish fruits.

Most parts of tutu are very poisonous and caused such severe losses in cattle and horses in the early days of settlement in Otago that surveyors and explorers noted its occurrence on their maps.

Tutu is found throughout New Zealand and is a plant of bush edges and streamsides. It is now a common roadside plant, which makes it particularly dangerous to driven stock.

Plate 9

cm

Karo

Pittosporum crassifolium Banks & Sol. ex A. Cunn.
Family: Pittosporaceae

KARO is a small tree from the northern North Island coast that has become naturalised in the warmer parts of the country. It grows to a height of 10m and has dark green leathery leaves backed with white. The flowers are a rich crimson and sweetly scented. In common with other pittosporums the capsules split open to reveal the dark seeds set in a sticky gum. The seeds are spread by birds, and various kinds of pittosporum seedlings quickly appear in the ground below places where birds congregate.

Karo is a popular garden plant because of its attractive habit and its ability to flourish in dry, windy places near the sea.

Plate 10

cm

Tarata

Pittosporum eugenioides A. Cunn.
Family: Pittosporaceae

TARATA or lemonwood is a handsome tree reaching a height of 13m. The foliage is a distinctive yellowish-green and the leaves are very shiny and fragrant with wavy margins. Tarata is spring flowering with sprays of starry, pale yellow flowers that are followed by small, dark capsules.

Tarata grows in open forest areas and along streamsides in most parts of New Zealand except for the south of the South Island and in dry areas.

Plate 11

cm

Ramarama

Lophomyrtus bullata (A. Cunn.) Burret
Family: Myrtaceae

RAMARAMA is a small, shrubby tree reaching a height of about 8m, although it is often much shorter. The foliage is a distinctively yellowish-green tinted with red or bronze when the trees are growing in full sunlight. The leaves are glossy and reflect the light on the raised and pouched surfaces between the veins. The rata-like flowers are white and are followed by dark red or blackish-purple succulent berries.

Ramarama is a plant of open forest often in places near the sea and extends from the far north to Marlborough and Nelson.

Plate 12

cm

Houhere

Hoheria lyallii Hook. f.
Family: Malvaceae

HOUHERE or mountain ribbonwood are pretty, deciduous trees with slender trunks reaching a height of about 10m. The foliage is a soft, greyish-green until the leaves turn yellowish in autumn. Mountain ribbonwood is abundant in the South Island mountains.

The form shown here is a plant of the wetter, western slopes formerly referred to as *H. glabrata* as it is less hairy than those growing in the drier mountains. Groves of mountain ribbonwood colonise stony slopes especially where avalanches and slips have cut a path through the tussocks and shrubs. The flowers are like cherry blossoms but are followed by dull, dry capsules.

Plate 13

cm

Manatu

Plagianthus betulinus A. Cunn.
Family: Malvaceae

MANATU, also called ribbonwood, (see previous page) is a deciduous tree which may reach about 20m in height. It is a tree of open places and is particularly common on alluvial soils on wide river plains. The trees are very conspicuous in spring when the new leaves are vivid green. The flowers are very small but are borne in large sprays at the ends of the branchlets. The fruit is a small beaked capsule.

Manatu grows throughout New Zealand in places where there is an adequate rainfall and a fertile soil, and is often seen on farmland.

cm

Putaputaweta

Carpodetus serratus J.R. & G. Forst.
Family: Escalloniaceae

PUTAPUTAWETA, also known as marble-leaf, is a small tree about 10m high with a slender, pale trunk and lacy foliage. The leaves are small and mottled in shades of green, with darker pigmentation along the veins. The flowers are small and white and are produced in abundance. They are followed by sprays of dark purplish, berry-like fruits.

Putaputaweta is a tree of forest margins and streamsides in forest throughout New Zealand. It often persists where the bush has been cleared for farming, particularly in shaded gullies and in second-growth forest.

Plate 15

cm

Tawari

Ixerba brexioides A. Cunn.
Family: Escalloniaceae

TAWARI is a beautiful tree of the northern forests where it is often found on the higher ranges in extensive groves. It grows to a height of about 15m with a pale trunk and branches and a spreading canopy of dark green foliage. The leaves are long, narrow and leathery and surround the clusters of creamy white flowers opening in late summer. The pointed fruit capsules split to show the shiny black seeds set in an orange flesh.

Tawari is found only in the north of the North Island, reaching its southern limit at the northern edge of the Volcanic Plateau.

Plate 16

cm

Dwarf Kowhai

Sophora prostrata Buchan.
Family: Papilionaceae

ALTHOUGH dwarf kowhai may become a slender tree up to 2m high in sheltered places it is mostly a very tightly branched shrub often dome-shaped or lying close to the ground. The branchlets bend almost at right angles and interlace; they may be leafless in dry situations and in winter. The leaves are small with only a few pairs of leaflets compared with the tree kowhais. The flowers are also small and have a bright orange flush on the largest petal. They are followed by a small, wingless pod constricted into only a few seed compartments each containing a large, dark brown seed. The pod is silky with fine hairs.

This unusual little kowhai was discovered by John Buchanan in the dry Awatere Valley. It is found in scrub and on dry tussocky hillsides in Marlborough and Canterbury.

Plate 17

cm

Kaikomako

Pennantia corymbosa J.R. & G. Forst.
Family: Icacinaceae

KAIKOMAKO is a small tree reaching a height of 12m, although it may be dwarfed in some of the exposed, windy sites where it is often found as a tough little tree with persistent, juvenile, rubbery, bent branches bearing small kite-shaped leaves. Kaikomako also grows in open forest or in forest margins and here the glossy, dark green leaves and the open sprays of small, white, scented flowers are better developed. The fruits are succulent, blackish drupes.

Kaikomako is found in forest and scrub from Northland to Foveaux Strait and Stewart Island.

Plate 18

cm

Matagouri

Discaria toumatou Raoul
Family: Rhamnaceae

MATAGOURI, a name derived from the correct Maori name, tumatakuru, is also widely known as Wild Irishman. It is a shrub or small tree which may reach a height of 6m, forming impenetrable thickets on hillsides, in gullies and over stony riverbeds. It may seem leafless in very dry places, but the leaves are small and bunched around the bases of hard, woody thorns that are set at right angles along the branches. The sweetly scented flowers encircle the branchlets and are followed by small, three-lobed capsules.

Wild Irishman is particularly abundant in the dry hill country of the eastern South Island. At a distance it has a distinctive purplish-grey colour, although many plants may be quite green where there is shade or shelter.

Wild Irishman was formerly found as a shrub in the lower part of the North Island, but it has now disappeared from some coastal localities where it was once plentiful.

Plate 19

cm

Orihou

Pseudopanax colensoi (Hook. f.) Philipson
Family: Araliaceae

ORIHOU or mountain five-finger is a low-growing shrub above the bush line or a small tree up to 7m in less exposed conditions. It clearly resembles five-finger (*P. arboreus*) but differs in having duller, thicker leaves with mostly unstalked leaflets which may be in threes or fives. The illustration shows the three-leaved variety in fruit and a leaf with 5 leaflets. Orihou has large sprays of greenish-yellow flowers followed by purple or speckled fruits.

Orihou is found in mountainous areas from Little Barrier Island to Stewart Island.

Plate 20

cm

Lancewood

Pseudopanax ferox Kirk
Family: Araliaceae

THIS uncommon lancewood is a slender tree reaching 7m closely related to the well-known lancewood or horoeka. Although of similar habit, the "ferocious" lancewood is immediately recognised by the hooked teeth of the juvenile leaves that are described in the Latin epithet "ferox". The mature leaves are smooth-margined and very thick and leathery.

Although this lancewood is rarely seen in the wild it is illustrated here because it is becoming widely planted in parks and gardens where it immediately attracts attention.

It is found in open forest or scrub areas in both the North and South Islands, but is considered to be rare and local in occurrence.

Plate 21

cm

Pate

Schefflera digitata J.R. & G. Forst.
Family: Araliaceae

PATE is a large-leaved shrub or small tree up to 8m high that is abundant in wet forest. The leaves are divided into 7-10 radially-arranged leaflets that are very thin and soft compared with the five-finger species. Pate has very small greenish flowers on large, branched inflorescences. The fleshy fruits ripen to violet.

Pate grows throughout New Zealand, mainly along streamsides and at the forest margin. It is especially common alongside tracks and roads.

Plate 22

cm

Inaka

Dracophyllum longifolium (J.R. & G. Forst.) R. Br.
Family: Epacridaceae

INAKA or grass tree is one of a number of species of *Dracophyllum* reaching tall shrub or tree size, up to 3m or more high, that are found in lowland or mountain scrub in various parts of the country. They have slender, rather stiff clusters of leaves with sheathing bases, branches ringed with the scars of fallen leaves and white flowers followed by brown, dry capsules.

The inaka illustrated is one of the most widely distributed as its range extends from the centre of the North Island to the subantarctic islands and from sea level in the south to the subalpine scrub.

Plate 23

Mountain Neinei

Dracophyllum traversii Hook. f.
Family: Epacridaceae

MOUNTAIN NEINEI is a striking tree with a most distinctive and beautiful pinkish-brown bark that comes away in strips. It grows up to 10m high and has widely spreading branches often set at a wide angle to the trunk and with large crowns of dark green to bronze tapering leaves. The large flower heads are produced from the centre of the leaf crown; the individual flowers are small and dark, wine-red. They are followed by cone-shaped clusters of reddish-brown capsules.

Mountain neinei is best seen in areas of high rainfall where roads ascend through mountain forest. The neinei usually grows at or near the upper limit of the forest in the more open places.

It is mainly found on the western side of the South Island, but in South Westland the single-trunked Fiordland neinei takes its place. In the North Island from the Coromandel Peninsula to the East Coast mountains, the neinei previously known as *D. pyramidale* is now considered to be the same as the southern mountain neinei.

Plate 24

cm

Tawapou

Planchonella novo-zelandica (F. Muell.) Allan
Family: Sapotaceae

TAWAPOU is a northern coastal tree reaching a height of about 10m with smooth, grey bark, glossy grey-green leaves and with stems yielding a milky juice. The flowers are small and insignificant, but they are followed by large, shining berries that change through shades of orange to purplish-black as they ripen. They contain one or more hard seeds that can be retrieved from beneath the trees.

Tawapou is found from North Cape to near East Cape on coastal hillsides and islands; it is a handsome tree that should be more widely grown in seaside gardens.

Plate 25

cm

Karamu

Coprosma robusta Raoul
Family: Rubiaceae

KARAMU is a Maori name also shared with *C. lucida* (see *Trees I*). The two species are rather alike; they both grow to a height of about 5m and have orange fruits, but those of *C. robusta* are smaller and more tightly clustered around the stems. The leaves are less shiny and sometimes turn a pronounced brownish-green in open scrubland.

Karamu is abundant in second-growth bush and along tracks and roads. In common with other coprosmas it is widely dispersed by birds.

Plate 26

cm

Taupata

Coprosma repens A. Rich.
Family: Rubiaceae

TAUPATA is a truly coastal tree or in many instances a low growing shrub. It is never found far from the shore and can withstand salt-laden gales. Plants from exposed places have conspicuously inrolled leaf margins, but where there is more shelter the shining leaves expand to their rounded "looking-glass" shape. Taupata will grow to a height of about 6m; it is an excellent hedge plant for seaside gardens and various forms with yellow variegations or bronzed leaves are popular garden plants. The fruits are clear orange and are very soon taken by the birds.

Taupata grows on the shore from the far north to Marlborough, Nelson and to near Greymouth in Westland. It is frost tender and does not flourish in inland areas.

Plate 27

cm

Tree Daisy

Olearia arborescens (Forst. f.) Ckn. & Laing
Family: Compositae

TREE DAISY is the most widespread of several small *Olearia* trees with white flowers that grow to a height of 5m or more. The leaves of tree daisy are bluntly toothed and angular with a glossy upper surface and silvery white beneath. The slender trunk is covered with pale, papery bark that peels away in thin strips. When the large sprays of pure white daisy flowers appear in late spring this tree daisy like the more northern heketara *(O. rani)* is immediately obvious amongst the greens of the surrounding bush. The flowers are followed by dull-brown fluffy seeds.

Tree daisy is found in open forest, scrubland and in coastal bush from East Cape to Stewart Island.

Plate 28

cm
mm

Tupare

Olearia colensoi Hook. f.
Family: Compositae

TUPARE or leatherwood is a small tree over 5m high in southern coastal areas, but on the mountains it is a short, very dense shrub. The trunks and branches are often contorted or flattened by gales and are covered with a pale, flaking bark. The leaves are tough and leathery with a white, felty undersurface. The leaf size varies according to the locality; tupare from the mountains has smaller, tougher leaves than the tupare fringing the coasts of Stewart Island and Fiordland. The flowers are clustered in dense purple heads followed by fluffy seeds.

Tupare in its several forms is found on the North and South Island mountain ranges and on the southern coasts.

Plate 29

cm

Hakeke

Olearia ilicifolia Hook. f.
Family: Compositae

HAKEKE or mountain holly is a small tree up to 7m high but is often much stunted in subalpine localities. The trunk and larger branches are clad in pale bark that comes away in hanging strips. The foliage is a light greyish-green and fragrant. The leaves are narrow and tough with sharply-toothed margins. The small daisy flowers are borne in large sprays during the summer and are followed by the fluffy seeds.

Hakeke is found from near East Cape, mainly in the mountain ranges, to Stewart Island. In some South Island localities — Arthurs Pass and the Hollyford Valley in particular — beautifully grown mountain holly trees may be seen at the roadsides.

Plate 30

cm

Koromiko

Hebe stricta (Benth.) L.B. Moore
Family: Scrophulariaceae

KOROMIKO is the Maori name for the shrubby and tree species in the large genus *Hebe.* The koromiko illustrated is the most widespread tall (up to 4m) tree koromiko found throughout the North Island to Marlborough. In the South Island and Stewart Island the very similar *Hebe salicifolia* is equally widespread.

Both these koromikos have slender tapering leaves and abundant white to pale lavender flower heads in late summer. The flowers are followed by small rusty-brown capsules. The North Island tree koromiko differs from the South Island one in the way the leaf edges meet in the upright, terminal leaf bud. The southern species has a small, shield-shaped gap (sinus) at its base while in the northern species the bud is tightly closed to the base.

The tree koromikos are plants of streamsides, forest margins and bluffs.

Plate 31

Puriri

Vitex lucens Kirk
Family: Verbenaceae

PURIRI is a massive tree reaching a height of 20m with a huge, pale-barked trunk and spreading limbs. The foliage is dark green and extremely dense; few plants are found in the shade of these trees. The leaves have a glossy surface that bulges between the veins. The flowers are rosy-pink and followed by cherry-like red drupes; both flowers and fruit (in varying stages of ripening) are found throughout the year.

Puriri trees that have been damaged or blown over soon develop new branches from the trunks and displaced limbs which accounts for the strangely contorted growth of ancient trees.

Puriri grows in coastal forest from North Cape to Taranaki and the Mahia Peninsula, and is common in parks and gardens south of its natural range.

Plate 32

For further reading

Flora of New Zealand, Vol. I H. H. Allan,
Vol. II L. B. Moore and E. Edgar,
Vol. III A. J. Healy and E. Edgar.

Eagle's Trees and Shrubs of New Zealand, Series One and Two, Audrey Eagle.

Rare and Endangered Plants of New Zealand, David R. Given.

The Oxford Book of New Zealand Plants, L. B. Moore and J. B. Irwin.

Trees and Shrubs of New Zealand, A. L. Poole and N. M. Adams.

The Native Trees of New Zealand, J. T. Salmon.

Stewart Island Plants, Hugh D. Wilson.

Native Trees I, Mobil New Zealand Nature Series, Nancy M. Adams.

In addition to the national park handbooks, the Department of Lands and Survey has now published illustrated brochures for many reserves and detailed vegetation surveys of three South Island National Parks — Mount Cook, Mount Aspiring and Westland.